Great
Fugue

Great
Fugue

Volker Braun

translated by Karen Leeder
and David Constantine

Smokestack Books
1 Lake Terrace,
Grewelthorpe, Ripon
HG4 3BU

info@smokestack-books.co.uk

www.smokestack-books.co.uk

designed by
Hermann Michels and
Regina Göllner, 2021.

First published
by Suhrkamp Verlag
Berlin
2021.

ISBN 9781739772222

Smokestack Books
is represented
by Inpress Ltd

Introduction

Volker Braun is one of Germany's foremost lyric poets. First in the German Democratic Republic (or former East Germany), where he began his literary career, and after 1990 in the Berlin Republic, he has published some eleven volumes of poetry to date most recently *Handbibliothek der Unbehausten* [Travelling Library of the Dispossessed] (2016). He has received numerous major awards for his writing: including the Bremer Literature Prize (1986), the Schiller Memorial Prize (1992), the German Critics' Prize (1996), the Erwin Strittmatter Prize (1998) and the prestigious Georg Büchner Prize (2000) awarded by the German Academy for Language and Literature. Recent years have brought international honours, including the Candide Prize (2009), appointment as Chevalier in the 'Ordre des Arts et des Lettres' (2012) and the Prix international Argana de la Poésie (2015). From 1999 to 2000 he was the Brothers Grimm Professor at the University of Kassel and he served as the Director of the Literature Section of the German Academy of Arts (2006–2010).

He began as a poet, and it is arguably his poetry that will be his most distinctive and long-lasting legacy. But he is perhaps almost better known, internationally at least, as a dramatist, novelist and essayist. His plays are frequently performed in Germany and beyond, including his recent classical plays *Demos, Die Griechen/ Putzfrauen* [Demos, The Greeks/Cleaning Ladies] (2016); his controversial *Unvollendete Geschichte* [Unfinished Story] (1975), or his *Hinze-Kunze-Roman* [Tom, Dick and Harry Novel] of 1985, following the adventures of a party hack and his chauffeur, remain brilliant and blistering insights into power relations within the socialist state. Equally, since 1990, his picaresque exposure of the inadequacy and indignity of welfare reform and back-to-work programmes *Machwerk oder Das Schichtbuch des Flick von Lauchhammer* [Botched or the Shift Book of Flick von Lauch-hammer] (2008) and particularly a number of shorter darkly satirical narrative pieces have carved out for him a central place in contemporary German literature. More recently his work journals have appeared in two volumes *Werktage I and II* (2009, 2014),

along with a book of aphorisms. Nevertheless, all Braun's texts are linked: drama, essays, novels and poetry all borrow from one another and form an organic whole that is bound up with Braun's life. Braun is a political poet in that from the beginning his work has been filled with rage, grief and a determined hope in the face of history in the making. But his poetry has also simultaneously always transcended national and political borders, seeking out the possibilities to be human in poems that insist on the love, humour, grief and beauty of the everyday world.

This volume appeared with Suhrkamp in Germany in May 2021. The central sequence of nine poems, 'Große Fuge' or 'Great Fugue', was written in March/April 2020 as a response to the global pandemic. The title is programmatic: hiding within it is the German 'FUG' the equivalent of the English term FUO (fever of undetermined origin), but also referencing Beethoven's 'Great Fugue, B flat major op. 133' rejected and reviled upon publication on account of its 'unintelligibility'. For Braun, the virus is something that causes humankind to reflect on its corporeality and its mortality, for sure: but it is also symptomatic of the global ecological-political crisis and is enmeshed in a broader philosophical and political context. In the Anthropocene, the Mekong can no longer find its delta, wildfires rage through parched forests, the world is in the grip of a 'War of the Landscapes'. And, in the middle of it all, humankind, so human and so transient, does what? It washes its hands. Characteristically, the intense, experimental poems cite a myriad of sources (some in English in the original), including Ezra Pound's *Cantos*, Shakespeare, Marx, Kleist, Imre Kertész, Braun himself (in a wealth of hidden self-citation), his fellow GDR poet Karl Mickel, as well as philosopher Rudolf Bahro, theorist Donna Haraway, Greta Thunberg, Angela Merkel and even Boris Johnson. This seems at times to be 'the conversation of the material with itself', as Braun puts it in one of the poems. A special place goes to Braun's GDR artist colleague Carlfriedrich Claus (1930–1998), whose artwork, 'Aggregate K', forms the subject of the longer final poem in that sequence. Braun is one of the most caustic of those writing on the left against what he sees as a kind of end-days scenario of late capitalism. The poems

are angry and often deeply ironic, mourning humanity's ongoing lack of what Marx called 'the dream of something of which it needs only to become conscious for it to possess it in reality' (Marx to Arnold Ruge, September 1843). Nevertheless, as often in his work, there are seeds of hope that come here from the young – mobilising in the teeth of ecological collapse – and from a philosophy of hope drawn from the utopian legacy of philosopher Ernst Bloch: 'It is still early morning politically'. The sequence of poems 'Clay Warriors' written in August and September 2020 goes back to a concern already evident in the poems written shortly after 1989 and Braun's first visit to China. These are more personal poems is some ways, haunted by death, the ailments of old age, illness and memory, and a moving final poem is situated among his fellow writers – the living and the dead – in the Dorotheenstadt Cemetery in Chausseestraße, Berlin. But here too is a link back to the 'haunted ship' of the second poem 'After our Time', a telling symbol of contemporary civilisation. But these poems also seek to wrestle with the origins of terror, transgender debates and theories of the posthuman. They all bear the imprint of Braun's passionate engagement in the times and in literature, and always set out to explore what it is to be human in the here and now. This volume contains the poet's own notes with additional references that might be useful for an English readership.

Karen Leeder, Oxford, 2022

Inhalt

I

  Wachtraum   14

  Nach unserer Zeit   18

II *Große Fuge. Aggregat K*

  Katarrhsis   22

  Windbürger   26

  Ginster. Plantagenet   30

  Palaver im Sand   34

  Der Aussätzige   38

  Schmerzgedächtnis   40

  Sorgen des Staatswesens   42

  Handschlag   46

  Aggregat K   48

III *Tonkrieger*

  Arbeitspapier   56

  Leibesbeweis   58

  Sechster Kreis   60

  K wie Kertész   64

  Anatomie. Kleist, Meinhof   68

  Kyborg   74

  Steinabreibung   76

  Große Leinwand   80

  Geisterstunde   84

Contents

Introduction   7

I
    A Waking Dream   15
    After our Time   19

II *Great Fugue. Aggregate K*
    Catarrhsis   23
    Wind Citizens   27
    Gorse. Plantagenet   31
    Palaver in the Sand   35
    The Leper   39
    Memory of Pain   41
    Cares of the Body Politic   43
    Handshake   47
    Aggregate K   49

III *Clay Warriors*
    Working Paper   57
    Bodily Proof   59
    Sixth Circle   61
    K like Kertész   65
    Anatomy. Kleist, Meinhof   69
    Cyborg   75
    Stone Rubbing   77
    Big Screen   81
    Hour of the Ghosts   85

Notes   88

I

I

Wachtraum

Seit langem träume ich nicht, das ist ein schlechtes Zeichen
(: ich arbeite auch nachts nicht), ich habe das Unterbewußtsein
verloren, Genossen, kein Homeoffice im Schlaf, die gewohnte
Schwarzarbeit. Nur ein Wachtraum stellt sich ein, der *Traum
von einer Sache*, die nicht in der Welt ist, oder einer Welt, die
nicht meine Sache ist. Ich liege im Bett, erkältet, schweißnaß,
und drücke die kahle Stelle am Kopf gegen die Wand. Ich sehe
drei übermannslange Raketen im Gelände, wir tragen sie weg,
sagt einer (ich), wir fassen vorn und hinten mit bloßen Händen
an. Die dritte ruht noch im Gras, aber ein Fremder taucht aus
dem Gesträuch und versteht sogleich, sich nützlich zu machen.
Wir schleppen die Schwucht ins Haus, das Haus der Kindheit,
und bugsieren sie auf das Doppelbett, ausgerechnet in meinen
Teil, er setzt sie ordentlich ab und streicht das Laken glatt und
schlägt das Deckbett halb über den Eisenleib. Ich bin unzu-
frieden, ich hatte mich von rechtswegen hineinlegen wollen, wir
sind schon wieder im Gelände und betten das Ding im Gebüsch
und laufen weg. Langer Marsch um den gesperrten Ort, ein
Mädchen schließt sich an, sie hat ein Kind aufgelesen. Der Junge
begreift, daß er zu schwer ist, von ihr getragen zu werden, und
blickt mich starr an. Doch mein Gewissen widmet sich der
Abteilung, die vorbeimarschiert, wir Zivilisten stehen ganz
ungünstig neben der Straße und weichen in einen Hohlweg, in
dem wir ungesehn weiterlaufen (in den Verhältnissen einfach
dabei). Hören eine Ansprache an in einem geklinkerten
Durchgang die Treppe hoch und wieder heruntersteigend.
Einmal herumgewälzt im Bett – und wir sitzen in Kalkstein-
brüchen im heißen Wasser und sehn die wie ein Tafeltuch
ausgebreitete Landschaft, an den Nähten der Felder die
Zypressenstiche. Die Piazza übrigens ein antikes Wasserbecken,
um das man nur herumsteigen kann, es ist verdreckt,
halb zugedeckt mit Blattgewächsen, nur zwei drei (Inder?)
stehen reglos darin. Ein Truppenrest Barbarossas, der die
Blessierten in die Schwemme schickt, bevor sie zum nächsten
Schlachthof ziehn. Die düstere Flüssigkeit (Blut?) vermutlich

A Waking Dream

It's a long time since I dreamed, that's a bad sign (: nor do I work at night), I have lost the sub-conscious, comrades, no Home Office in my sleep, the usual moonlighting. Only a waking dream has put in an appearance, the *dream of a thing* that is not yet in the world, or not in a world that is my business. I'm lying in bed, with a cold, drenched in sweat, and I press my bald spot against the wall. I see three rockets, longer than a man is tall, on the site, one of us (me) says let's carry them away, we'll take hold of them either end with both hands. The third rocket is still lying in the grass but a stranger pops up out of the bushes and sees at once how to make himself useful. We drag the deadweight into the house, the house of childhood, and manoeuvre her onto the bed and it *would* have to be on my side, he lays her down carefully, smooths the sheet and pulls the cover half way up over the iron body. I'm not happy, I had wanted to lie down myself as it was my right to, we are back on the site again, we put the thing to bed in the bushes and run away. A long march around the locked-up place, a girl joins us, she has picked up a child. The boy realizes he is too heavy to be carried by her and stares fixedly at me. But my conscience is taken up with the unit marching by, we civilians are standing very awkwardly by the road and we retreat into a hollow way in which we can continue unseen (easy enough in the circumstances). We listen to an address in a clinkered passage climbing and descending the stairs. Turned over once in bed – and we are sitting in limestone fissures in hot water and see the landscape spread out like a tablecloth and along the seams of the fields the stitching of the cypresses. The piazza actually an antique basin which you can only climb around, it is filthy, half covered with foliage in which only two or three (Indians?) are standing motionless. A remnant of Barbarossa's troops, he is sending the wounded into the watering place before they move on to the next slaughterhouse. The dark liquid (blood?) doubtless from the

aus den Fleischfabriken, Halbpension unter dem Abendhimmel für Schweinegeld. Oben am Rand des Prospekts ein Brand, der sich in den trockenen Wald frißt, der fuchtige Wind facht eine weiß und braune Rauchsäule an. Und die Brände im Schanzenviertel, der schwarze Block, Polithooligans & *20 000 Beamte*, vulgo Notwehr gegen strukturelle Gewalt. Mescalero die Rothaut meldet sich wieder mit einer indianischen Weisheit: *nur noch für die Ungewißheit auf die Straße gehen.* Und wieder umgedreht das nasse Kissen und weitergewachträumt. Snowden kommt den Hang herunter am Mauerstreifen aus dem Gefängnis (nach meiner Lebenszeit), ein alter gelöschter Mann, der den Kindern hinter der Hand vom Datengestöber erzählt. Er hat sich auf die Wetterbeobachtung verlegt, die Wolkenwäsche (Datenwolken!), und erinnert sich als einziger an Westhofen, Workuta und Rohwedder, vergessene Gegenstände. Was treibt die Menge hier, was stellt sie dar, wer sind die kaschierten Köpfe. Wie bei den Fernsehgeräten versteht man die Worte nicht mehr, verkommene Technik (für die verkommene Öffentlichkeit). Ich murmle was wie *morgen wiederzukommen*, allein, und mit einem Einzelnen zu sprechen, und man sagt mir, daß ich nur seinen Kopf fassen und ihn mit den Händen reiben müsse. Währenddessen teilen Dealer Verpflegung aus, jede achte Büchse Speed

meat factories, half board under the evening sky for a small fortune. On the top edge of the view there's a fire eating into the dry forest, the furious wind is fanning a white and brown column of smoke ahead of it. And the fires in the *Schanzen-viertel*, the black cell-block, political hooligans *& 20,000 civil servants*, that is, in common parlance, self-defence against structural violence. Mescalero the redskin shows up again with some Indian wisdom: *take to the streets now only in the cause of uncertainty*. And another turning over of the wet pillow and the waking dream continues. Snowden comes down the slope along the wall out of prison (not in my lifetime), an old and extinguished man who whispers to the children about the blizzard of data. He has shifted to weather-watching, cloud-washing (clouds of data), and is the only one who still remembers Westhofen, Vorkuta and Rohwedder, forgotten subjects. What's the crowd up to here, what do they stand for, whose are the concealed heads. As with the television sets, we don't know what the words mean anymore, a debased technology (for a debased public). I mutter something like *come again tomorrow*, alone, and to speak with one person, and I'm told all I have to do is take hold of his head and rub it with my hands. Meanwhile dealers are distributing provisions, every eighth box is speed

Nach unserer Zeit

EINE WEISSE YACHT DER MAST GEBROCHEN BEWE-
GUNGSUNFÄHIG VOR MINDANAO DÜMPELND EIN
KÖRPER FAHL UND BRÜCHIG WIE DRECKIGER
FEUCHTER SAND ZUSAMMENGESUNKEN AM TISCH
NUR NOCH IN FORM UND HALTUNG EINEM MEN-
SCHEN ÄHNLICH
So sehe ich die Menschheit treiben
In ihrem Fahrzeug Nach ihrer Zeit
Totenstille Ein Geist ist an Bord

After Our Time

A WHITE YACHT ITS MAST BROKEN
UNABLE TO MOVE ROLLING OFF
MINDANAO A CORPSE PALE AND
FRAGILE LIKE DIRTY WET SAND
SLUMPED AT THE TABLE ONLY IN
ITS SHAPE AND ATTITUDE RESEMB-
LING A HUMAN BEING
Thus I see humanity drifting
In its conveyance After its time
Deathly quiet A ghost is on board

II
Große Fuge
Aggregat K

II
Great Fugue
Aggregate K

Katarrhsis

Die Stadt ist ruhiggestellt
                    wie ein Pestpatient
Ein Morgenfrieden bis Mitternacht
Entmenschte Straßen, wie befreit
                    von der Krätze
Der Kunden. Der Senat schließt die Kneipen zu
Die Stadien verwaisen BLEIERN UNION. Die Museen
Den Marmor-
                    mumien, die Theater den Geistern
Halt. Wer da / Nein, antworte du mir
Nicht vor Publikum, nicht in dieser Saison.
Platzangst Flachatmung Katarrh im Kulturbetrieb, einmal
All dem (Unfug) Einhalt gebieten EIN JAHR OHNE KUNST
So kommt Ruhe ins Verfahren, ihr Dilettanten.
Auch die Tafel
                    ist dichtgemacht,
                              eine Schutzmaßnahme
Aber *having none* (Habenichtse) *hath no care to defend it.*
Die Kanzlerin rät von sozialen Kontakten ab
Streifenwagen
                    schaun nach, ob noch Leben ist
Was haben Sie 2020 gemacht? – Die Hände gewaschen
Kein Shakehands, doch vorsichtshalber der deutsche
Gruß. Der HErr zieht den Finger zurück in der Cappella Sistina
Damit er sich nicht ansteckt
            ·   in der Risikogruppe
Der Überalten, jeder vierte (Gott) stirbt.

Catarrhsis

The city is sedated
                    like a plague patient
Morning peace till midnight
Unpeopled streets, as if freed
                              from the scabies
Of custom. The Senate closes all the pubs
The stadiums orphaned LEADEN UNION. Museums
For the mummies
                  of marble, theatres for the ghosts
HALT. WHO'S THERE / NAY, ANSWER ME
Not before an audience, not this season.
Fear of confinement Shallow breathing Catarrh in the culture
    industry,
Put a stop to the (mischief) once and for all A YEAR WITHOUT ART
That will bring some decorum to proceedings, you dilettantes.
Even the soup kitchen
                      has been shut down
                                          a protective measure
But *having none* (have-nots) *hath no care to defend it.*
The Chancellor advises against social contact
Squad cars
          prowl in search of signs of life
What did you do in 2020? – I washed my hands.
No *Shakehands*, but as a precaution, the German
Greeting. The LORD withdraws his finger in the Sistine Chapel
To avoid infection
                    in the high-risk group
of the very old, one in four (gods) dies.

Ein Schatten streift dich bloß, ein fahler Hauch
Touchiert deine Lungen, du atmest durch
Im Anthropozän
           The scientists are in terror
And the European mind stops (Canto CXV)
China schwitzt das Übel im Schwitzkasten aus
Ein Unterarmwürgegriff (: in die Armbeuge husten)
Lernt, Kontinente, die Lava kochen

A shadow passes over you simply, a sallow breath
Grazes your lungs, you're still breathing
In the Anthropocene
       The scientists are in terror
And the European mind stops (Canto CXV)
China sweats the evil out in a headlock
A forearm choke (: cough into your elbow)
Learn, you continents, to cook lava

Windbürger

Windige Leute, gierig nach Luft in den Lungen
Auf kahlen Kuppen, Brachland, brandenburgischer Steppe
Ein alternativer Lohnerwerb unter sausenden Rädern
Wie wenn am Feiertag
              ein Landmann auf sein Spargelfeld geht
Das in den Himmel ragt, und sein hochgehaltnes Gezähe
Arbeitet, ohne sein Zutun,
              ein Zubrot, das im Wind wächst

Oder am Werktag die Werktätigen vor ihrem Werk
Standen andächtig, im Regen,
              auf die Grundmauern starrend
Oder die leeren höhnischen Hallen
Das Weltende: der Plan, war erfüllt
Vorfristig im Osten

Lange ging er mit sachtem sicherem Schritt
Der Mann unter Bäumen.
              Jetzt tappt er gott-
Verlassen im Asphalt umher, und wo sind die Vögel?
Und nicht Mutter Natur hält ihn
              allgegenwärtig, in leichtem Umfangen
Das Sonnenlicht weckt keine vergangenen Freuden auf.
Der Kostgänger der Jahreszeiten, auf ihre Milde
War Verlaß, jetzt steht er im Wetter-
              wandel, Weltenaufruhr
Er ist durch den Wind, die Zyclowne regieren ihn
Ein Virus ist stärker als er, ein Schleim ohne Stoffwechsel
»Nach heutiger Definition kein Lebewesen« und schon bald
   eine Gesellschaft
Der grüne Grashelm hat dich ausgestochen

Wind Citizens

Windy folk, fly by nights, greedy for air in their lungs
On bare hilltops, fallow land, Brandenburg steppe
An alternative income under the rushing turbines
As when on a holiday
                  a farmer walks out to his asparagus field
That towers into the sky, and his upheld miner's toolkit
Works, of its own accord,
                  a nice little earner, that grows in the wind

Or on a workday the workers stood before their work,
Reverently, in the rain,
                  staring at the foundations
Or the empty, scornful factory floors
The end of the world: the quota was achieved
Ahead of time in the East

For years he walked with a soft and certain tread
The man among the trees.
                  Now he gropes about, God-
Forsaken in the asphalt, and where are the birds?
And Mother Nature does not hold him
                  all-present, with a light embrace.
The sunlight wakes no past joys to new life.
Lodger of the seasons, whose gentleness
Could be relied upon, now he stands in the weather-
                  change, upheaval of worlds
He came through the wind, the cyclowns rule over him
A virus is stronger than him, a mucus without metabolism
'Not a form of life, according to current definitions' and all
   too soon a society
The green casque has outdone your elegance

Ein Flügelschlag

Legt ihn um, the climate of history

Und du läufst, ein panisches Freitagskind
In der Begängnis im Weltgebäude
                    aus der Geschichte
Kein Telos, »eine Handvoll Maximen«
                    und ein Trampelpfad
Aus den Systemen. Das ist deine Kunst jetzt
Allein zu sein, mit allen, und ernst
Auf dich gestellt wie der Stein, der Halm
Und mitzudenken mit den Gebirgen und Meeren.
Nur einen Sommer haben wir noch vor es Winter wird.
Ihr Ölbäume Kretas, dreitausendjährig, ihr mächtigen
Gletscher. Sieh das Übrige an,
                    die holozänen Bestände
Hoffnungs-
        trägerin, Artgenossin
»Wie könnt ihr es wagen« –

                                        One flap of a wing
Lays him flat, *the climate of history*

And you run, a panicked Friday's child
In the funeral business of the world edifice
                                        out of history
No *telos*, 'a handful of maxims'
                              and a beaten track
Out of the systems. That is your art now,
Being alone, with everyone else, to shift
For yourself in all earnest, like the stone, the stalk
And think things through with mountains and with seas.
Just one more summer left to us before it is winter.
You olive trees of Crete, three thousand years old, you mighty
Glaciers. Look at what is left,
                              the holdings of the Holocene
Our hopes
            pinned on her, fellow member of our species
'How dare you' –

Ginster. Plantagenet

Britannische Küsten, gelbleuchtend, büsche-
                                                                bewehrt
Sichtschutz bei der Jagd und Augenweide
Ein Graf von Anjou, den Zweig am Helm, *plante genêt*
Fing den Namen ein
                                Und nachfolgend Richard of York
Ein Königreich für tausend tote Pferde,
                                                das Ginster-
Geblüt. Neunzig Arten; Ginster, aus der Nähe, stinkt
Spesenritter, expense knight, Bastarde und Bluthunde
Die Blankverse sprechen
                                Dialekt der Natur
Und Unnatur, ein haltbarer Spielplan. *Scene – the Globe*
Das Gerücht *tritt auf, ganz mit Zungen bemalt*
Und spricht von Schuld
                                Waldfrevel Waschzwang Luftverletzung
Die Unzucht der Schlachthöfe
                                        und Unschuld natürlich
Familiendramen mit Mord-Werkzeugen, zwangsläufig
Im Badezimmer, das Bauernlegen der Banken

Über die Böschung gebeugt, seh ich sie reiten
Gelbleuchtend, zwischen den Büschen
Verrückte, die Visiere/Schädel geöffnet
Das Rostbeef Europas. Ein Rohrbruch her
                                                Die S̶i̶n̶t̶-
Die Sinnflut ins Trockendock der *Civilisation*:
Ein Brettspiel von F.G. Tresham (from 13 years)
Der Nach-Wuchs setzt sich in Bewegung, die boden-
Ständige Erde, ausgeholt wie sie ist,
                                        spielt mit uns *production*

Gorse. Plantagenet

Britannic coasts, shining yellow, bulwarked with
                                                    bushes
Hunters' cover and sight for sore eyes
A Count of Anjou, sprig on his helmet, *plante genêt*
Caught hold of the name
                                    And after him Richard of York
A Kingdom for a thousand dead horses,
                                        the gorse-
Bloodline. Ninety varieties; gorse stinks close-up
Knights of the expense-fiddle, bastards and bloodhounds
The blank verse speaks
                            the dialect of nature
And Un-nature, a tenable repertoire. *Scene – the Globe*
Enter Rumour, *painted full of tongues*
Speaking of guilt
                        forest offences ablutomania air violations
The corruption of the abattoirs
                                    and innocence of course
Family dramas with instruments of murder, in the bathroom,
Inevitably, the peasant clearance of the banks

Leant over the embankment, I see them riding
Shining yellow, between the bushes
Madmen, their visors/skulls open
The roastbeef of Europe. A burst pipe ago
                                        The ~~deluge~~
The delusion of reason into the dry dock of *Civilization:*
A boardgame by F. G. Tresham (from 13 years)
The off-spring are on the move, this grass-
Roots earth, poised as it is,
                                plays *production* with us

Mit ihren Ressourcen Zonen Gezeiten
Früh- und Spätschicht bis zum Verrecken. Wir
Die Reservearmee im Krieg der Landschaften:
Die Rosenkriege
                Wollt ihr sehn, was ein Weltkrieg ist
WELCOME IN THE KOM-POSTMODERNE
Said Donna Haraway. Und umgebettet die grauen
Gräber in die Zusammenhänge

Exit old mankind.

With its resources zones tides
Early- and late shift till the death of us. We
The reserve army in the War of the Landscapes:
Wars of the Roses
                    You want to see what a world war is
WELCOME TO THE COM-POSTMODERN
Said Donna Haraway. And the grey graves
Are re-interred into the relations

Exit old mankind.

Palaver im Sand

Madame hebt den Fuß aus dem Meer, die schwarze Sohle
Färbt die Sandale, Oleandertaler
Am Persischen Golf. Warm warm ist das Wasser
Wo die Truppen landen, reisende GIs
Und DJs
            und reisige Dichter in Saadiyat Island

»Er kann Arabern Sand verkaufen«: kein Witz
Und den Amerikanern Demokratie (that too)
Sie bleiben auf ihren Wüsten sitzen. Kein Baumaterial
Für diese versinkenden Türme, zu denen man
Als wären sie weißwas, aufblickt. Ogott
Die Sandhändler sieben die See aus,
                            den Futon der Meere
Das Bett der Flüsse weggezogen im Schlaf. Der Mekong
Ausgelöffelt, findet sein Delta nicht mehr
Und Sand rinnt, wie Öl, in die Briefkastenfirmen

Sand was my youth and my work, werfe ich ein
: Sand und Kies Schluff Letten, *Material Burghammer*
Sand war der Sinn und Unsinn, das mittel-
Deutsche Loch *Ausgekohlte Metapher*
Keiner Mutter Boden Loser Satz
                     (wir wußten nicht was wir hatten)
»Wärst du gegangen, Idiot«
                  And that is my new land, ein
Morgenland wirklich, in den Sand geschmiegt, und was siehst du
Schimmernd, vom Flugzeug aus?

Palaver in the Sand

Madame lifts her foot from the sea, the black sole
Stains her sandals, Oleander valleys
In the Persian Gulf. Warm warm is the water
Where the troops land, travelling GIs
And DJs
          and mounted poets on Saadiyat Island

'He can sell sand to the Arabs': no joke
And democracy to the Americans (that too)
They stay sitting on their deserts. No building material
For these sinking towers, which one looks
Up to as if they were something special. Oh God
The sand-dealers are sieving out the sea,
                                   the futon of oceans
The beds of rivers stolen in their sleep. The Mekong
Spooned out, cannot find its delta any more
And sand runs, like oil, into the offshore companies

Sand was my youth and my work, I interject
: Sand and gravel silt loam, *Material Burghammer*
Sand was the sense and nonsense, the central
German hole *Metaphor Cleared of Coal*
Of no Mother Ground Less Sentence
                         (we did not know what we had)
'If you had gone, Idiot'
                    And that is my new land, a
True morningland, huddled in the sand, and what can you see
Shimmering, from up there in the plane?

Windräder wieder
In Windeseile verbreitet, ansteckend, ein Ausschlag
Global, die Leiharbeiter der Lüfte
Streiken sie? fliegen die Fetzen? Die Wolken-
                                gewerkschaft
Läßt sich nicht kaufen für ein Trinkgeld von E.ON. Natur-
Gesetzliche Ruhepausen für
                        die nah am Wind gebaut sind
Alle Räder stehen still
Wenn der starke Wind nicht will

Ein Areal nackter Sand einen Steinwurf landein
Ein Schrebergarten, wo der Buchscheikh hofhält
In seiner weißen Kandura, in einem grünen Zelt
Tiefgekühlt wir eingesunken in die sandigen Sofas

                              Wind turbines again
Spread like wildfire, contagious, a global
Rash, the contract workers of the airs
Are they on strike? Will sparks fly? The union of
                                        clouds
Won't let itself be bought for small change by E.ON. Rest
     breaks
According to the laws of nature for
                              those built close to the wind
All the turbines stand still
When the wind won't blow

An area of bare sand a stone's throw inland
An allotment, where the Book-Sheikh holds court
In his white kandura, in a green tent
Refrigerated, and us sunk into the sandy sofas

Der Aussätzige

Ich sah Bahro wieder, in Worms. Er ging ohne Mundschutz
Seit Bautzen, er war immun; während wir uns in Selbsthaft
   verfügten
Wer bist du? rief ich. – Noch einmal ein Mensch, er lachte
   befreit:
Im Übergang –
              Es waren ihm Flügel gewachsen
Und er trug Kissen mit sich für die Meditation
Vor der Megamaschine. Ausgebremst war sie auf sein Geheiß
Die Aeroplane vom Himmel geholt, und pünktlich fallen die
   Züge aus
Das Leben zwangs-
              entschleunigt, »nur noch ums Haus herum«
Geht die Logik der Rettung, »das Nichtstun bringt es«.
Wie sie bewegt ist, miteinmal, stillezustehn,
                        die Welt
Wie zur Besinnung gebracht. »Das Naheliegende birgt das
   Geheimnis«
So fuhr er fort
          Die Alte, ausgemergelt, dement
Schrie uns vom Kaufland zu: Pandemie
Lacht und schlägt um sich mit dürren Armen, rastet aus
Und St. Rudi umarmte sie furchtlos, sein Schweißgeruch
Und andre Vorsicht rissen mich rückwärts, froh doch
Dem Kumpel wiederbegegnet zu sein in besseren Zeiten.

The Leper

I saw Bahro again, in Worms. He hadn't worn a face covering
Since Bautzen, he was immune; while we were busy self-
   imprisoning.
Who are you? I called. – A human being again, he laughed
   relieved:
In transition –
               He had grown wings
And he carried cushions with him for meditation
Before the mega-machine. On his orders it had ground to a halt
Planes plucked out of the sky, and trains are cancelled punctually.
Life is slowed
          by decree, 'only close to home'
Runs the Logic of Salvation, 'doing nothing is the key'.
How it is moved, all at once, to stand still,
                         this world
As if brought to its senses. 'The obvious harbours the secret'
He continued.
         The old girl, gaunt, demented
Screeching at us from Poundland: Pandemia
Laughing and flailing around with withered arms, going berserk
And Saint Rudi embraced her without fear, the smell of his sweat
And other kinds of caution tore me back, though glad
To have met my old mate again in better times.

Schmerzgedächtnis

Es war eine erste Berührung,
                              ich scheute zurück
Wie ein Füllen.Von ihrem Hals, oder war es
Die Wange, ich weiß es nicht mehr, der Mund

Gut, ich gebe den Kuß zu. Niemand sah uns
Den Kuß, aus dem, warum, nichts folgte
Es waren normale Zeiten, angstlos zeigte man
Das nackte Gesicht. Es ist so lange her, dreißig, drei Jahre
Ich sehe noch genau ihr helles dünnes Kleid, aufgeknöpft
Von meinen Händen. Ich fuhr zurück, eine Scheu
In Kindertagen im Körper
                              bewahrt

Ihre Nüstern zitterten noch, sie hielt mich fest
Auf dem Steinweg, ich trabte hinab. Jetzt in den Zeiten der Pest
Wir trügen Masken, beide
Fest über Nase und Mund, der gehauchte
Kuß zungen- und zahnlos zärtlich
                              mit vorsichtshalber
Auch geschlossenen Augen. Es wäre leicht.

Memory of Pain

It was a first touch,
                    I shrank back
Like a colt. From her neck, or was it
Her cheek, I no longer recall, the mouth

OK, I confess the kiss. No one saw us
That kiss, from which, though why, nothing came to pass
These were normal times, we showed our naked faces
Without fear. It is so long ago, thirty years, three
I can still see her light thin dress, unbuttoned
By my hands. I stayed back, a shyness
From childhood days, stored
                            in the body

Her nostrils still quivered, she held me tight
On the stone path, I trotted down. Now in times of pestilence
We'd be wearing masks, both of us,
Tight over nose and mouth, the breathed
Kiss without tongues or teeth tenderly
                            and, as a precaution,
Our eyes shut too. It would be easy.

Sorgen des Staatswesens

Die Wesen sehn das Staatswesen an. Es ist ernst
Geworden. Was kommt auf uns zu?
Man sieht nichts, und sie lachen, lästern
Trinken Bier. Der Staat geruht zu regieren
Soviel Wesens sonst um nichts, Routinen Bluff
In den Parlamenten. Es ging um die schwarze Null
Er hat lange nicht nachgedacht, nichts zurückgelegt, keine
Gedanken gehortet. Nicht einmal das Klopapier
Das sie wert ist. Jetzt darf er Mittel in die Hand nehmen
In beide Hände die Bevölkerung ersuchen etc. etc.
Jetzt spricht die Queen. Boris Johnson
Liegt auf der Intensivstation bzw. es geht ihm besser
Die Büste des Perikles steht im Office, Downing Street 10
Der Stratege, der bevor er den Krieg in Attika lostrat
Die Bürger zwischen die Langen Mauern einlagerte
Wo sich im Gewühl der Tod breitmachte. Seine zwei Söhne
Erlagen der Pest, auch Perikles. Boris denkt
Er habe das Beste noch vor sich
                              Ein gewöhnliches Wesen
Fragt im Radio: wie lange geht das schon so?
Daß ein beinahe heilloser Stillstand herrscht,
                              und sich wies scheint
Nur die Gewinn- und Verlustmaschine dreht
Ohne erkennbaren öffentlich-kulturellen Sinn? – Die Athener
Ließen sich Theatergeld und Kornspenden ausschütten.
Meinem Wesen entspricht
                    seh ich das da
Daß ich Abstand halte und auf Anfrage twittere:

Cares of the Body Politic

The bodies look at the body politic. Things just got
Serious. What's coming down the pike?
Nothing to be seen, and they laugh, curse
Drink beer. The state deigns to rule
So much ado about nothing else, routines bluff
In the parliaments. A question of breaking even.
It has not thought hard for a long time, has put nothing aside,
Kept no thoughts back. Not even the toilet paper
That would be worth the stake. Now it can take things in hand
In both hands, call on the people etc. etc.
Now the Queen will speak. Boris Johnson
Is in intensive care; either that or he's on the mend.
A bust of Pericles stands in his office, Downing Street,
    number 10.
The strategist, who stashed the citizens behind the Long Walls
Before he unleashed the war in Attica
Where in the turmoil death held sway. His two sons
Victims of the plague, Pericles too. Boris thinks
That the best still lies before him
                              A common creature
Asks on the radio: how long has this been going on?
That we're at an almost unholy standstill,
                              and as it seems
Only the machine of profit and loss keeps turning
Without any obvious public cultural sense? – The Athenians
Got their theatre their money and grain handouts.
In accord with what I am
                    as I see it
I keep my distance and und tweet on request:

Ich bin
        nicht der
Und meine Billigung
                    ihr
          habt   nicht. Wir
    wissen nicht was   werden können.
              wir
Aber es gibt natürlich ausführlichere Metren
Für Worte wie mitleiden-
                schaftlich, gemeinsüchtig
Menschenmöglich, wenn es uns ernst wird
Was reden, was denken wir hin –
Mehr als wir denken sind wir
                    sagte Einer kurz-
Angebunden

I am
        not him
And my endorsement
                        you
        is something   do not have. We
        don't know what   can become.
                        we
But naturally there are more elaborate metres
For words like suffering com-
                        passionately, yearning for a common cause
the humanly possible, when things get serious.
Where are we heading in our words, our thoughts –
More than we think, we are
                        said someone – out of
The blue

Handschlag

Das Wesen, das sich die Hand gibt (seit wann? die Römer
Etrusker), befangen oder emphatisch, *zivilisiert*
Wird aussterben,
        weiß Wallraff, der verdeckte
Enthüller, also das Abendland geht ohne Abschied
Ein Winkewinke, das wars. Man kann sich verneigen
Wie auf einer höfischen Bühne, Regietheater, der Einfall
Einander nicht zu berühren,
        MeToo-Ästhetik, correctness
Der Jetztzeit

        Ich sitze am Tegeler Fließ
Mein Vaucluse. Laura am anderen Ufer, nicht zu durchwaten
Das Wasser, *ein grüner inwendiger Wald*, durchströmt
Von Canzonen. Ich halte die Pfote hinein –
        die Hand
Die nach der Frucht greift, nach dem Werkzeug, die rettende
Die sich ausstreckt zu dem überladenen Boot
Im Tyrrhenischen Meer, und eine Hand ergreift. Faß zu
Halte sie fest in deinem Vers
        Und der sagenhafte
Handschlag, velkommen, im Rathaus, der Eingebürgerten
Danmarks.

Handshake

The creature that offers another its hand (since when? Romans
Etruscans), awkward or emphatic, *the civilised one*
Will die out,
                    says Wallraff, the undercover
Whistleblower, that's to say the Western World is off without
        a word
One quick bye-bye, that was it. One can take a bow
Like on a stage at court, Regietheater, the idea being
Not to touch each other,
                            MeToo-aesthetic, correctness
Of the here and now

            I sit by the Tegel stream
My Vaucluse. Laura on the other bank, this water not
For wading, *a green inwardly wood*, streaming
With canzoni. I dip my mitt in –
                            the hand
That reaches for the fruit, the tool, the saving hand
That stretches out toward the overcrowded boat
In the Tyrrhenian Sea and grasps another hand. Grab it
Hold it tightly in your verse.
                            And the fabled
Handshake, *velkommen*, in the townhall, of the naturalised
Citizens of Danmark.

Aggregat K

Ein Gerät, verrostet verdreckt unbrauchbar gemacht
Ein Strommast vielleicht, Metall und Gebein
Verworrener Draht ummantelt mit Blut
                                    Das Bild-
Material alter Zeiten, in die Landschaft gesunken
Verwitterte Losungen, rätselhaft
Die Wikinger? Moskowiter? Beim Nähertreten
Sperrgebiet: da geht kein Gespenst mehr um
Vermint womöglich, jedenfalls nicht geheuer

Claus hat es gezeichnet ganz als Schrift
»Unleserlich«, auf transparentem Papier
                                    beidseitig
Gegen das Licht zu halten, das EINST UND JETZT
Feder Pinsel Finger Kreide z.T. Reißungen
Das Aggregat Erinnerung Traum Der Gang in den Schneewald
Bewußtsein
            die »ewige Frage« nach dem Unrecht schlechthin
Schwarze Fahnen, der Totenstrom im Hirn

Etwas summt noch klirrt hallt nach in dem Kasten
Mit der Aufschrift K
                    Ein Geräusch aus Kavernen
Knochenschutt, ein Atemziehn, und pumpt
Sekrete wäßrige Fäden Fermente Sporen
Von Widerstand, aufgewehter Mut
Verzweiflung, das Springkraut aus der untersten
Erde und die Restkraft der Kontinente

Aggregate K

Some contraption, rusted and filthy, rendered unusable
A pylon perhaps, metal and bones
A muddle of wire crusted with blood
                              Image-
Stock of bygone times, sunk into the landscape
Weatherworn slogans, inscrutable
The Vikings? Muscovites? Approaching now
Prohibited zone, no spectre haunts it any more
Possibly mined, certainly eerie

Claus has drawn it all as writing
'Illegible', on transparent paper
                         both sides
To be held up to the light, the THEN AND NOW
Pen paintbrush finger chalk in parts just tears
The Aggregate Memory Dream A Walk through the Forest Snow
Consciousness
                  the 'eternal question' about injustice per se
Black flags, the stream of the dead in your brain

Something still hums rattles echoes in the box
With the label K
                  A sound that comes from caverns
Bone debris, a drawing of breath, pumping
Secretions watery threads enzymes spores
Of resistance, courage lifted up
Despair, exploding balsam sprung from the deepest layers of
Earth, and the last strength of the continents

Er sah mit Augen Zunge Zahn, *sah durch*
Auf die Spiegelschrift, Zukunft (von VORN UND HINTEN), un-
Erledigt. 　　Das Gespräch des Materials mit sich selbst
»Das Verhältnis etwa der chinesischen Tusche
Zu Metall oder Folie und ihre Reaktion auf Äthanol«
Das Gedächtnis eines entschlossenen Strichs
Oder weiß schwarz »brutal überdeckt was da steht«

Arbeit) »der Stoffwechsel mit der Natur«
Mit der geringsten Kraft organisiert; die unmittelbar auf die Not
Des andern bezogene Handlung, nicht vermittelt
Durch ein Äquivalent; Gemein-
Sinn und -besitz DAS IST DER KERNBEREICH DER FABRIK
Mitleiden-
　　　　schaftlich, gemeinsüchtig, eine mögliche
Praxis, *um die sich alles wie um die Sonne dreht*

Liebe) Er übte sie, keusch wie ein Kämpfer
　　　　　　　　　»auf dem Weg Ho Chi Minhs«
Der / dem Entfernten nah sein / sich, kein qiángjiān, kein
shōuyín,
　　　　(das flüsterte mir schon Jin auf den Wällen Xi'ans)
Seis drum, er gewann Kraft
Die kleinen Orgasmen zwischen den Wörtern (Eva Hesse ad Pound)
Die Sanfte Kunst, mit der leeren Hand
　　　　　　　　　fechten

He saw with eyes tongue tooth, *saw through*
To the mirror-writing, future (from FRONT AND BACK), un-
Finished.
        The conversation of the material with itself
'Like the relationship of Chinese ink
To metal or foil and its reaction to ethanol'
The memory of a decisive line
Or white black 'brutally covering what is there'

Work) 'metabolic exchange with nature'
Organised with the lightest touch; action related
Directly to the need of the other, not mediated
Through an equivalent; common
Cause and -ownership THAT IS THE CORE AREA OF THE
    FACTORY
Suffering com-
          passionately, yearning for community, a possible
Praxis, *about which everything revolves as about the sun*

Love) He practised it, pure as a warrior
                  'on the path of Ho Chi-Minh'
Who being close to him/her who is distant, him/herself, no
    qiángjiān, no shǒuyín,
             (as Djin whispered to me on the walls of Xi'an)
Be that as it may, he gained strength
The little orgasms between the words (Eva Hesse ad Pound)
The Gentle Art, of fencing with an empty
                 hand

Haltestellenschilder = Steckbriefe, im
Ehem.Werksgelände. Unterbewußte Felder
Resttexte, ggf. Bombentrichter. Folgen
Die Robinsonaden
                    des Überflusses. Klärschlamm
Die Verheißung, praktisch vom Mund abgespart. Ihre schräge
Gestalt sitzt noch am Weg, eine Verrückte, nackt
Vor der Wahl, vor Scham zu versinken / weiterzuwandern
Mit ihrem Geheimnis Schwäche Rotz Anarchie
In andere Dünen, Dürregebiete, *Brüder zur Sonne*

»Es ist noch früher politischer Morgen«
Er drückte die Hand auf das Blatt, »auf die Geschichte«
Aus dem Solarplexus heraus jäh beschleunigt
Der Karate-Schlag aus dem Augenblick,
                                      der sie ingangsetzt
Dem gehenden Fuß geht der Boden auf –

Stopsigns = wanted posters, in
Former factory sites. Unconscious fields
Leftover texts, poss. bomb craters. Now follow
The Robinsonades
                    of superfluity. Sewage sludge
The promise, practically scrimped out of nothing. Its strange
Shape still sits by the roadside, a lunatic woman, naked
Faced with the choice of dying of shame / walking on
With her secret – weakness snot anarchy –
Into other dunes, regions of drought, *Brothers, to the sun*

'It is still early morning politically'
He pressed his hand onto the page, 'onto history'
From the solar plexus suddenly speeds
The karate-blow from the moment
                                that sets it in motion
For the foot as it walks, the ground opens up –

III
Tonkrieger

III
Clay Warriors

Arbeitspapier

Wie es aussieht, ist das meine letzte Arbeit
Schreibt mein junger Neffe Evolution und Gesellschaft
Ein *Entwurf*. Die Therapien sind fehlgeschlagen
Schmerzen Die Sache nimmt Fahrt auf. Er war noch immer gelassen
Seinen Tod im Leib und das Leben noch vor sich
Das Arbeitsamt schickte ihn als Hilfskraft zur Heilsarmee
Die ihm bescheinigte, nicht zu brauchen zu sein. Er ging
Ins erschwingliche Exil, »auf Mark Aurels Boden«, nahe Gran
Kein Thema abhandeln einen Denkstil finden
Vor allem keine Konsistenz, wenn es um Wahrheit geht
Die Welt ist ein Fragment. Vielleicht lassen sich die Rätsel
Nur auflösen, wenn er in Rätseln spricht Leider verstehe ich nichts
Von Quantenphysik Der Beobachter ist Teil und Akteur
Im beobachteten Ereignisbereich (am Rand der Gesellschaft)
Eine Wissen- und Tatschaft »für Heller und Pfennige«.
Das ungebundene ist sogleich das glücklichere Denken
Es wird nicht schaden, Natur und Kultur als Fließgewässer
Zu betrachten/behandeln Statt der großen Begradigungen
Da und dort ein Damm mal ein Polder, im allgemeinen
Dem Fluß seinen Lauf lassen. So reden Cäsaren
Und underdogs im Drogenrausch Ein ununterbrochener
Wechsel und damit eine besondere Art Gleichförmigkeit
Problem und Lösung, Katastrophe und Aufbruch
Eine lange Epoche ungewohnter Unordnungen.
Natur&Kultur: Die biologische Selektion greift
Die Individuen an, die kulturelle betrifft Produkte
Verhältnisse Ideen etc., ohne daß zwangsläufig, sagt er
Menschen geopfert werden müssen Ich selbst bin ein gutes Beispiel
Als jemand der im biologischen Kampf schon verloren hat
Den aber die Medizin am Leben hält. Er vertraute darauf
Daß ihn die Medikamente, wenn es zu Ende geht
Im Moment kommt mir alles wie ein Abenteuer vor
Nicht wie eine Bedrohung, betäuben Was geschieht
Ist eigentlich ganz alltäglich

Working Paper

The way it looks, this will be my last piece of work
My young nephew writes Evolution and Society
A *draft*. The therapies have failed
Pain The thing is accelerating. He was still unperturbed
Death in his body and life ahead of him
The Job Centre sent him to the Salvation Army as an assistant
And they certified they had no use for him. He went
Into an affordable exile, 'Marcus Aurelius country', near the Granua
Not to treat a topic to find a style of thinking
Above all no consistency if it's about truth
The world is a fragment. Perhaps the riddles
Will only be solved if he speaks in riddles Alas I have no
    understanding
Of quantum physics The observer is a part and an agent
In the observed range of events (on the edge of society)
Science and the deed of it, 'down to the last penny'.
Coming undone is itself the happier thinking
It won't hurt to view/ treat nature and art
As running waters Instead of the large straightenings
Here and there a dam, now and then polder, on the whole
Let the river go its way. So speak caesars
And underdogs in the drug-rush An uninterrupted
Changing and so a particular kind of uniformity
Problem and solution, catastrophe and outset
A long era of unaccustomed disorders.
Nature&Culture. Biological selection
Attacks individuals, cultural affects products
Circumstances ideas etc, without necessarily, he says
Requiring people to be sacrificed I am myself a good example
As someone already defeated in the biological struggle
But whom medicine keeps alive. He trusted
That the medicaments, when the end comes
At the moment everything feels like an adventure
Not a threat, will anaesthetize him Really
What's happening is commonplace

Leibesbeweis

Nicht oft kommt es vor, daß ich ihm Liebe zeige
Nachlässig wie ich bin faul und gefühllos
Gerade dem Nächsten gegenüber, der Körper
Ist es gewohnt und wird nicht gewartet
Eine Durchsicht im Halbjahr Routine, nicht mal entkleiden
Muß man sich bei der Ärztin, Puls und Schritte
Zählt das Handgelenk, in der Seele sind keine Sensoren
Um ihren Zustand beiläufig abzufragen.
Die einzige Abnormität ist ein um Kilometer zu langer
Darm, weshalb der Abflat keinen Ausweg findet
Das ist das zentrale Problem, erzähle ich zerstreut
Ich habe da Frau Doktor einen besseren Zugang
Aber ganz allgemein nicht das Herz dazu. Es liegt
Vielleicht an den verdickten Herzkammerwänden, verhärtet
Von *Schwerarbeit* (kommentiert die Notaufnahme), die mir
Gar nicht bewußt ist. Zumutungen Schikane
Erklären die Kollegen, die mich an die Maschine
Anschließen, fehlende Zuwendung kann man sagen, ich selber
Wüßte nur eine, gar nicht verwerfliche, Handlung
Welche freilich zu selbstbezogen erscheint.

Bodily Proof

It doesn't often happen that I show him any love
Careless as I am lazy and unfeeling
Especially towards my nearest, the body
Is used to it and not looked after
An inspection every six months Routine, no need
Even to get undressed for the doctor, the wrist counts
Pulse and pace, in the soul there are no sensors
To ask in passing what state it's in.
The only abnormality is a kilometres-too-long
Intestine so that the waste can't find a way out
That's the main problem, Doctor, I tell her
Distractedly, I've got a better way in there
But generally don't have the heart for it. Perhaps
On account of a thickening of the ventricle walls, hardened
By *heavy work* (a note made at my emergency admission) that I
Am quite unaware of. Insults Harassment
Colleagues explain, attaching me
To the machine, not enough loving care, you might say, myself
I can think of only one not at all reprehensible act
Which, it is true, seems too self-centred.

Sechster Kreis

Als wir die Weltenmitte durchgestiegen
An der Bornholmer, wo die Lücke klaffte
Wars Vorsatz oder Zufall, bin ich mit der
Neugierigen Menge bei den Antipoden.
Wirsamt wie aus der Stickluft vorgetreten
Die mir betrübt so Brust als Augen hatte
Der ganze Morgenhimmel lacht' im Glanze.
Das erste was mein irrer Blick erfaßt ist
Der Blätterwald, von dem ich lange träumte
Der Zeitungskiosk mit den Meinungsblättern
Und ich begreif, daß ich mich läutern solle.
Ein Fegefeuer also, aus den Akten
Wir wissen wohl, daß dir der Glaube fremd war
Der Mangel bleibt das Brandmal auf der Stirn
Wo man auf Einsicht wartet (: abonniert ist)
Um aufzusteigen aus der kargen Sphäre.
Zum Kreis der Schlemmer! und die Gier und Hab-
Sucht hebt mich in das sechste Stockwerk
Merkwürdig mager ist man hier kahlköpfig
Wir sehn uns an: bin ichs? sind wir es? wie
Dante die Verbraucher vorgesehn hat.
Nicht ins Elysium, ins Illuseum
Hat mich der Weg und allesamt geleitet
Soweit bis hierher Und nun weiter
Comandante. Und ich sah die Stange
Grün belaubt, in der Stadtmitte. Der Platz
Hiroshima die Zeit: danach Ein Alter
Der länger angewurzelt stand, trat
An meine Seite, mir die Welt erklärend
Was siehst du? einen Mast, er war ein Baum
Und ist es noch Und nur er überlebte
Von seiner Art, d.h. allein der Stamm

Sixth Circle

When we have climbed through the centre of the earth
At the Bornholmer where the gap opened wide
Was it by destiny or chance, I am with the
Curious crowd at the Antipodes.
All of us as though emerging from air we could not breathe
Which had clouded my vision and my heart
All the morning sky was laughing in the brightness.
First thing my distracted eyes take in:
The leafing forest of the press I have long dreamed of
The newspaper kiosk with opinion-sheets
And I understand that I must purify myself.
So: purgatorial fire, from the documents
We know full well that faith was a stranger to you
What's missing is the mark branded on the forehead
Where you wait to be enlightened (: are a subscriber)
To climb up out of the barren sphere.
Into the circle of the bon vivants! And lust and
Covetousness lift me onto the sixth floor
Remarkably skinny people here, bald-headed
We look at one another: is that me? is that us?
So Dante foresaw the consumers.
Not into Elysium, into Illusium
The way has led me and all of us
Thus far. And now onwards
Comandante. And I saw the pole
Leafing green in the city centre. The place
Hiroshima, the time: after An old man
Who had stood a long while rooted there
Stepped to my side, explaining the world to me
What do you see? A mast, it was a tree
And still is And it alone survived
Of all its kind – that is, only the trunk

Die Äste alle weggeloht von solcher
Glut die Menschen schmilzt. Und: fragte ich
Woher aber das Grün? – Die Blätter nämlich
Sprossen aus der schwarzen Rinde. Wir
Schwiegen vor dem ganz entmenschten Denkmal
Wie davon sprechen, Ann. – »Die süße nicht
Und bittre, aber feste Sprache.« – Der Baum
Unsrer Erkenntnis, sagte sacht der Alte
Dessen Ohren auch vom Stamm gehaun warn
Wie ich sah die Blicke senkend

Flames took the branches, in such heat
Human beings melt. But, I asked
How come the green? – Yes, the leaves
Sprouted from the black bark. We
Were silent before this memorial wholly without humanity
How should we speak of it, Ann. – 'Not the sweet
And bitter, but steadfast language.' – Our Tree
Of Knowledge, said the old man softly
Whose ears were also hewn from the trunk
As I saw, lowering my eyes

K wie Kertész

12. Oktober Der Nobelpreis ist wieder vergeben worden
Nicht an ihn In der Straßenbahn *das entschiedene Gefühl*
Nicht unter Menschen zu sein. Dann fiel mir ein, daß doch gerade
Diese Menschen die »neuen Menschen« sind, eine noch nicht
Dagewesene Art. Unglaubliche Brutalität Feigheit Herden-
Dumpfheit. Mordlust, die auf das erste Zeichen von Schwäche
Reagiert. Ich dachte, es sei ein menschlicher Instinkt daß
Wenn jemand zuboden geht, der Mensch zurückschreckt, womöglich
Aufhilft. Es steht außer Frage, daß die Welt zugrunde geht
Sagt K in Auschwitz geboren Wir sitzen im Diekmann
Meinekestraße beim Spargelessen.Worin besteht die Katastrophe
Sinniert er Wie soll man die apokalyptischen Taten
Erklären Auschwitz, der Gulag Hochentwickelte
Gesellschaften. Die Geschichte, daran ist kein Zweifel
Findet für nichts eine Erklärung. Er darf es sagen
Der in Buchenwald wohnte *Bei Beethoven kündigt sich*
Die Katastrophe an, in der Gebrochenheit der Fugen ... Brecht
Ein banal denkender und mittelmäßiger Schriftsteller
Der an die soziale Ungerechtigkeit denkt, was zu den
   schrecklichsten Verbrechen führt.
Ich hasse ihn, wenn er spricht Die tägliche
Gymnastik eines Clowns, der sich dem Haß entgegen-
Stemmt *Wie mag es sein zu leben, wo man dir Liebe*
Er schluckt, *oder zumindest wohlwollende Gleichgültigkeit*
   entgegenbringt?
Am Ku' damm also nicht in der Budakeszi, Fischsuppe
Spaghetti mit Muscheln. Ich zum Beispiel, sagt er
Bin unglaublich flexibel – ich bin nirgendwie *Dieser Mensch*

K Like Kertész

12 October. The Nobel Prize has been awarded again
Not to him On the tram *the decided feeling*
Of not being among human beings. Then it occurred to me
That precisely these are 'the new human beings', a species
Non-existent till now. Unbelievable brutality cowardice herd-
Insensateness. Lust to kill by the first sign of weakness
Quickened. I thought it was human instinct that if someone
Fell to the ground a human would be shocked, if possible
Help. Beyond dispute, the world is going under
Says K born in Auschwitz We are sitting in Diekmann's
Meineke Street, eating asparagus. In what does the catastrophe
   consist
He wonders How are the apocalyptic deeds
To be explained Auschwitz, the Gulag highly developed
Societies. History, beyond any doubt
Cannot explain anything. He is permitted to say this
Who lived in Buchenwald *The catastrophe is announced*
In Beethoven, in the brokenness of the fugues ... *Brecht*
A banal thinker and mediocre writer
Who thinks of social injustice, which leads to the most
   appalling crimes.
I hate him when he speaks The daily
Gymnastics of a clown setting himself against
Hatred *What might it be like to live where love*
He swallows, *or even just benign indifference is shown you?*
So not on the Ku'damm in Budakeszi, fish soup
Spaghetti with mussels. I myself, for example, he says
Am incredibly flexible – I am nowhere near like *This person*
Is capable of anything The catastrophe person
For whom there is no return to his centre.
This ego-less being is the real evil and amusingly

Ist zu allem fähig Der Mensch der Katastrophe
Für den es keine Rückkehr in seinen Kern gibt.
Dieses Ich-lose Wesen ist das wahre Übel, und amüsanterweise
Ohne daß es selbst schlecht wäre zu jeder Untat fähig
Immer noch wissen wir nicht was uns treibt und warum wir
Leben. *Auschwitz setzt sich fort überall in allem*
Er hat das Recht es zu sagen, K der *Auschwitzclown*
Es gibt Sätze die falsch sind, notierte Nietzsche
Die aber gesagt werden müssen. *Der Schmutz sprudelt*
Aus der Gesellschaft wie aus einer Kloake Er
Darf alles sagen. Es muß unbedingt
Gesagt werden Es ist empörend, es ist das Leben
Sagt der Überlebende, der nie aus dem Lager herauskommt
Auschwitz hat stattgefunden und
Was stattgefunden hat beeinflußt alles was noch stattfinden kann.
In ca. vier Jahren möchte ich sterben Richtig gelebt
Hab ich bis 1990. Glücklich war ich sieben Jahre 1983 bis 89
Mein Schreiben dient nur insoweit mich darzustellen
Wie dieses unbestimmte konturlose Wesen – ich –
Das Chaos darstellt. Morgendämmern Die klaren Konturen
Berlins wie von Nebel verwischt, in der Tiefe
Ein Leuchten Das ist das Sein selbst

Without itself being bad capable of any atrocity
We still don't know what drives us and why
We are alive. *Auschwitz continues everywhere in everything*
He has the right to say it, K the *Clown of Auschwitz*
There are, Nietzsche noted, sentences that are wrong
But which must be said. *The muck wells up*
Out of society as out of a cess-pit He
Is allowed to say anything. It must without question
Be said It is outrageous, it is life
Says the survivor, who will never get out of the camp
Auschwitz took place and
What has taken place influences everything that can still take place.
In four years or so I should like to die I really lived
Till 1990. I was happy for seven years 1983 to 1989
My writing serves only in so far to represent me
As this indefinite contour-less being – I –
Represents chaos. First light of morning The clear contours
Of Berlin as though wiped away by fog, in the depths
A lightening That is Being, the thing itself

Anatomie. Kleist, Meinhof

Wenn du die Welt nicht mehr im Kopf aushältst
Und den Irrsinn nicht mehr buchstabieren willst
Rate ich dir, beim nächsten dreckigen Anlaß zu handeln
Träumt Kleist in seiner WG am Wannsee
Was nicht heißt auf einen allgemeinen Widerstand warten.
Vielmehr sollst du allererst mit ihm beginnen
Normalerweise reicht ein Polizeihund, der in die Hosen beißt
Für die Aufwallung des Bluts, und die Bekanntschaft
Mit dem Gummiknüppel macht den ruhigen Fußgänger
Der seine Meinung vor sich herträgt, zum aufsässigen Element.
Diese einmal junge schöne Person, klar denkend/träumend
War berühmt in (geistig) gut situierten Kreisen für ihre
Kolumnen in *konkret*, für das ich wohl gerne geschrieben
Hätte, die sie allmählich
Zuspitzte wie mit dem Federmesser, dergestalt, daß die
   Herrschenden
Die sprachlose unverfrorene statische Macht
Sprich das System, hätten verletzt sein müssen.
Aber nichts, die Macht spricht nicht
Sie läßt sich in kein Gespräch verwickeln
Die sprachlose unverfrorene statische Macht, man mußte
Endlich die Regeln verletzen und ins Freie gehen
Wo die Steine fliegen. *Die Straße ist vielleicht kein so guter Ort*
Und ein Kaufhausbrand an und für sich kein Fanal
Das sich rechnet – hohe Haftstrafen
Schwer zu vermittelnde Motive, das Morden in Vietnam –
Das Progressive am Kaufhausbrand ist der Gesetzbruch
Lese ich als Stückeschreiber mit Interesse
Und der Appetit kommt beim Essen, der Heißhunger
Kommt wenn der Ofen brennt. Nicht, als ob damit
Etwas erreicht wäre, auf das es ankommt

Anatomy. Kleist, Meinhof

When you can no longer bear the world in your head
And no longer wish to spell madness, I advise you
At the next filthy cause to act, so Kleist
Dreams in his commune on the Wannsee
Which does not mean wait for some general resistance.
Much better you be the very first to begin it
Normally a police dog biting your trousers will suffice
To get your blood up and making the acquaintance of
A rubber truncheon will turn the peaceable pedestrian
Delivering himself of an opinion stroppy.
This once beautiful young person, clear thinker/ dreamer
Was famous in (intellectually) well placed circles for her
Columns in *konkret* for which I myself should have liked
To write, which she gradually
Sharpened as with a penknife so that the rulers
The speechless insolent state power
That is, the system, needed injuring.
But nothing, Power doesn't speak
Won't be drawn into any conversation
The speechless insolent state power in the end
It was necessary to break the rules and move into the open
Where stones are flying. *The street is perhaps not such a good place*
And a department store fire in itself not a beacon
That counts – lengthy prison sentences
Motives hard to get across, the murdering in Vietnam –
The progressive thing in the department store fire is breaking the law
As a dramatist I read that with interest
And l'appétit vient en mangeant, you're ravenous
When the oven's on. Not that anything
Of what needs doing was achieved by it

Aber wie ich doch irgendeine Vorstellung habe
Die mit dem was ich will von fern eine Verbindung hat
So schafft, wenn ich nur dreist den Anfang mache
Das Handeln, im Zwang weiterzugehn, Tatsachen.
Dabei ist nichts heilsamer als das Eingreifen
Der Staatsmacht, und ein sonderbarer Quell der
Begeisterung für den der handelt liegt
In den Physiognomien hinter den Plexiglasschilden.
Mancher Tatmensch weiß im Moment
Wo er zur Tat schreitet nicht, was er vorhat, aber
Die Umstände selbst und die daraus resultierende Erregung
Reißen ihn vorwärts, wie wenn in der Kleistschen Flasche, sic!
Strom generiert wird. *Die allmähliche Verfertigung*
Des Terrors beim Handeln. Konkret betrachtet
War auch dieses Blatt konterrevolutionär
Wie alle, denkt Kleist, *Berliner Abendblätter*
Und die erste rohe Aktion galt dem eigenen Schreibtisch
Röhl rief die Polizei. In dem Schweinesystem
Könnte man sagen, ging der Mann fremd
Und fickte zwischen französischen Stichen
In der Jugendstilvilla. Praktisch auf eigne Faust
Und ohne redaktionellen Auftrag sah sie dem Racheakt zu
Der Verwüstung der eigenen Wohnung, zumal
Der Ruinierung des Ehebetts durch ihre jungen Genossen
Selbst sie eine Ruine. Sie zog sich aus der Affäre
Aus den Affären in die Frontstadt Berlin
Wo längst gehandelt wird. Als der nach dem Brand in der Zeil
Inhaftierte Baader, auf dem Freigang befreit
Im Zentralinstitut für soziale Fragen
Ein Angestellter schwer verletzt am Boden
Den Abflug machte, folgte sie ihm durch das Fenster
Kurzschluß in den Synapsen, hinab in den Untergrund
Jetzt war das Blut geleckt und sie imstande
Unsichtbar wie sie ist, selbstlos zu handeln
Besinnungslos, also außer sich, ein Handeln

But how in this way I do get some idea
Remotely connected with what I want
If I at least make a bold beginning, action
Creates, in the compulsion to go further, facts.
And in that, nothing is more salutary than the intervention
Of state power and a strange source of
Inspiration for one who acts
Lies in the physiognomies behind the plexiglass shields.
Many a man of action at the moment when he moves
To act does not know what he intends but
The circumstances themselves and the excitement arising from them
Drag him forwards as when in a Leyden jar
Electricity is generated. *The gradual production*
Of terror in the act. Looked at concretely
This paper too was counter-revolutionary
Like them all, Kleist thought, *Berliner Abendblätter*
And the first violent act was against your own writing desk
Röhl called the police. In the corrupt shambles
We might say the man was unfaithful
And fucked among French engravings
In the *Jugendstil* villa. Pretty well on her own initiative
And with no editorial brief she watched the act of revenge
The trashing of her own flat, especially
The ruining of the marriage bed by her young comrades
Herself a ruin. She withdrew from the affair
From the affairs to the front-city Berlin
Where for a long time there had been action. When Baader
Arrested after the fire on the Zeil, freed in the hall
Of the *Zentralinstitut für soziale Fragen*
One employee seriously wounded on the floor
Made his escape, she followed him through the window
Short-circuit in the synapses, down into the underground
Now she had tasted blood and was in a position
Being invisible, to act selflessly
Thoughtlessly, in fact beside herself, actions

Dem kein Ich mehr dazwischenkommt
Banküberfälle Sprengstoffanschläge das herrlichste
Zugleich und höllischste Handeln *Angst ist reaktionär*
Das Drexperiment, wo die Schußhände wie Froschschenkel
  zucken.
Vor Gericht, an Armen und Beinen hereingetragen
Ließ sich die Person nicht mal zur Person vernehmen
Die Worte der Witz die Zunge herausgezogen
-gestreckt, die Kolumnistin zwanghaft verstummt
Vor der *sprachlosen Macht*, eingesperrt im selbst-
Gewählten Aus, vulgo der Tote Trakt, die
Teilnehmende Beobachterin in der Isolationshaft.
Die Obduktionsbefunde wurden nicht vorgelegt
Hier die Narbe am Hals. Die Stricke jedenfalls
Und brieflichen Aufforderungen sich aufzuhängen
Ließ der Vorsitzende Richter Prrinzzing
In die Zellen der Verbleibenden passieren, *feste Stricke*
Wurde protokolliert, geeignet dem Wunsch der Bevölkerung
Nachzukommen.

No Self would now interfere with
Bank robberies, dynamitings, actions
At once most splendid and most hellish *Fear is reactionary*
The experiment in filth where the hand holding the gun
    twitches like frogs' legs.
In court, carried in by the arms and legs
The person would not even permit her person to be questioned
Words Jokes sticking her tongue stuck out
The columnist compulsively saying nothing
In the face of *speechless Power*, locked up in self-chosen
Out of Play, in plain language, the Dead Zone, the
Sympathetic observer in solitary confinement.
The findings of the post mortem were not produced
The scar here on the neck. The ropes however
And the letters suggesting they might hang themselves
Were delivered by order of the Presiding Judge Prrinzzing
To the survivors' cells, *strong ropes*
It was recorded suitable to answer the wishes
Of the public.

Kyborg

Wie darf ich dich ansprechen, Freundin? *mein lieber*
Schwan mit der Schweißnaht, aus dem Ausbeßrungswerk
Eine Scheinschwangerschaft, extra-uterin
Guter Hoffnung (»auf das Ende der Unterdrückung«)
Die dich dir gebiert. Das Ein und Andere
Regellos, nicht von Kategorien erfaßt
Das ein Vielfaches ist, ausfransend fadenscheinig
Fluid
       Donna Haraway *macht sich ein Vergnügen daraus*
Den Körper neu zu lesen in seinem
Ironischen Kleid aus Seide und Blech. Der Tanz
Auf dem Gendergraben, Ost- West- und Zygoten
Die über die Grenze gehn den Mauerstreifen.
Sie sieht, wie weiße amerikanische
Männer sich am Computer animalisch gebärden aus
Haß aus Eifersucht auf die Maschine Aber
Warum sollte der Körper an der Haut enden oder
Nur aufnehmen, was in Haut genäht ist, z.B.
Mich der nicht aufgibt, deine Haut zu berühren?
Unlust, Niemandes Schlaf zu sein Oder
Wie die Rose der reine Widerspruch
Das Geschlecht mit einem Sprechakt ändern
Aber die Welt nicht, die trans-
                atlantischen Amazonen
Auf der Auffahrtsrampe zur Überwindung des Fleisches.
Bin ich noch in meinem Haus? fragt der Dichter &
Hauptmann in Schlesien, bevor der Waggon
Der Reichsbahn mit dem Toten beladen wird Bin ich
Noch in meinem Leib, morst der Maschinenmensch
In seinem lebensverlängernden Technolook.
Ein Urmensch, Mähne, gebückter Gang such ich
Am Strand ein Ersatzteil für die Evolution
Angespült von einem Schiffbruch, ein Werkzeug
Für die Liebe, ein lebendiges Ding wie den Tod.

Cyborg

How may I address you, friend? *my dear*
Swan with the welding seam, from the improvement works
A phantom pregnancy, extra-uterine
Expecting ('to the ending of oppression')
Which bears you to yourself. The One and the Other
Without regulation, not able to be categorized
That is a multiple thing, fraying threadbare
Fluid
      Donna Haraway *takes pleasure in*
Reading the body again in its
Ironic dress of silk and tin. The dance
On the grave of gender, East – West – and zygotes
Which cross the frontier the strip along the wall
She observes how white American
Men at their computers behave like animals out of
Hatred out of jealousy of the machine But
Why should the body end at the skin or
Only take up what is sewn up in skin, e.g.
Me who never stops touching your skin?
Reluctance, to be nobody's sleep
Like the rose, the pure contradiction
To change sex with a speech-act
But not the world, the trans-
                      atlantic Amazons
On the ramp ascending to victory over the flesh.
Am I still in my house asks the poet &
Captain in Schlesien before the Reichsbahn's
Wagon is loaded with the dead man Am I
Still in my body, the machine-man speaks morse
In his life-lengthening techno-look.
An *Urmensch*, a mane, stooping walk I'm searching
Along the beach for a spare part for evolution
Washed in from a shipwreck, an implement
For love, a living thing like death.

Steinabreibung

Große Wolken vollkommen ruhig Am Boden
Streicht Wind. Meister Zhao sitzt in der Schreibstube
Über den wie in Stein gehaunen Sätzen
Den Kronzeugen seiner Anklage, betr.
Alle bisherige Weltanschauung. Die Verfasser
Sind versammelt (zusammengerollt in den Regalen)
Kant, Papiergesicht und Packpapiersprache
Sieht sich verstohlen um, wo ist die Brechstange?
Des berüchtigten Nachdenkers und Verunsicherers
Vom oberen Perlfluß ... Hobbes & Konsorten
Haben ihre Abreibung weg, und der deutsche Idealismus
Sieht blaß aus. Kant Immanuel wird respektvoll behandelt
Immerhin habe er, Kant, den ewigen Frieden
Gedacht in Königsberg, Preußen Kein Nationalstaat.
Wo ist Ihr Königsberg, Kant, sagt Zhao
In seinem hölzernen Sessel Königsberg eine Vision
Wie vom Ruinenmaler Robert *Die Decke ist durch*
Im Louvre. Königsberg – Kaliningrad, leider – Kantgrad
Sagt Zhao, Ihre Welt ist gescheitert. – Kant:
§ 7 Grundgesetz, handle so, daß die Maxime deines –
Deines! Willens, du Einziger – jederzeit als Prinzip einer –
Gesetzgebung, lächelt Zhao nachsichtig Ihr ewiger Frieden
Ist ein ewiger Krieg. Auch der große Hobbes
Sann auf Frieden und redet vom Kampf aller / alle.
Oder Locke: die Konkurrenz, Marx: Klassenkampf
Schmitt: Freund / Feind. Das ist keine Welt
Die eine Welt ist. Alle unter einem Himmel
Sagten die Alten. – Kant breitet die Arme, hebt
Dann aber lieber die Stimme: Der gestirnte Himmel

Stone Rubbing

Large clouds perfectly peaceful On the ground
There's a wandering breeze. Zhao, the Master, sits in his study
Over the propositions which look hewn in stone
The principal witnesses in the charge he has brought concerning
Every world-view to date. The authors
Are foregathered (rolled up in the racks)
Kant, paper face and the language of wrapping paper
Looks surreptitiously around him, where is the jemmy?
Of the notorious thinker and unsettler
From the upper pearl river ... Hobbes & Co
Have had their rubbing, and German Idealism
Looks wan. Kant Immanuel is treated with respect
He, Kant, did at least give thought to perpetual peace
In Königsberg, Prussia Not a nation state.
Where is your Königsberg, Kant, Zhao asks
In his wooden chair Königsberg a vision
Like one of Robert's ruins *There is a hole in the ceiling*
In the Louvre. Königsberg – Kaliningrad, alas – Kantgrad
Says Zhao, your world is a failure. – Kant:
Para. 7 Fundamental Law, act only according to that maxim
By which your – Your! will, you one and only – always as the
     principle of –
A legislation, Zhao smiles indulgently Your perpetual peace
Is a perpetual war. Even the great Hobbes
Pondered over peace and speaks of the war of all against all.
Or Locke: competition, Marx: class struggle
Schmitt: friend/ enemy. That is not a world
That is a world. All under one sky
Said the Ancients. – Kant opens his arms, raise
Your voice then instead: The starry heaven

Über mir und das Sittengesetz in mir. – Immer
Im Unendlichen liegt die globale Gerechtigkeit Sie
Gehen unter dem geteilten Himmel, Himmanuel.
Tianxia setzt a priori die Welt als Ganzes voraus. –
Tianxia, buchstabiert Kant Aber die Kategorie
Aus dem Altertum klingt nebulös, ein Wellness-Gefühl
Aus der Zhou-Zeit, und auch die Jetztzeit Xis
Ist eine gefressene Kreide-Zeichnung
Dreißig Dynastien, wie lang ist das her? – Null, sagt Zhao
Wie vom Westfälischen Frieden zum Weltkrieg
Und wendet sich dem Vollbart zu, der sein ebenfalls
Gescheitertes Konzept der Aufhebung der Klassen
Unfroh hochhält, exklusiv sozusagen
Proletarier aller Länder ... – Koexistierende Produzenten
Erwidert Zhao, *all-inclusiveness*. Mehr Konsequenz, Marx
Jetzt bewegen sich die Wolken In der Kammer Windstille
Brecht, den er aber fürchtet, hängt als Rollbild
An der Wand, *Der Zweifler*, kein Kronzeuge
Und fragt: Wer baut das torlose Theben?
Ist nicht wenigstens eine KP dabei? Und
Wo bleiben, wenn die Große Mauer geschleift ist
Die Abrißarbeiter?

Above me and the moral law within me. – Global
Justice lies forever in the infinite. You
Walk beneath the divided sky, Celestial Immanuel.
Tianxia supposes a priori the world to be a whole.
Tianxia, Kant spells it But this category
From antiquity sounds vague, a Wellness-Feeling
From the Age of Zhou, and even the present Age of Xi
Is a worse-for-wear chalk drawing
Thirty dynasties, how long ago is that? – Zero, says Zhao
From the Peace of Westphalia to the First World War, as it were
And turns to the Beard who unhappily holds up
His likewise failed concept of the dissolution of the classes
Exclusively, we might say
Workers of the World ... – Coexisting producers
Zhao replies, *all-inclusiveness*. More rigour, Marx
Now the clouds are moving In the Chamber, no wind at all
Brecht, whom he is afraid of, hangs as a scroll
On the wall *The Doubter*, not a principal witness
And asks: Who builds gateless Thebes?
Is there not at least a CP there? And where
When the Great Wall is demolished
Will the demolition men be left?

Große Leinwand

Wie ein kleines ungeordnetes Reich, dieser Künstler
Im Jahr 76, Scheidung Auszug das Chaos Aber ein Fürst
Kann seinen Wohnsitz wechseln, Frankenhausen
Ein Großauftrag *Frühbürgerliche Revolution*, d.h.
Eine Epoche malen (das war die Maßeinheit)
So daß die Bevölkerung in das Bild hineinpaßt.
Der Rundbau steht wie eine Falle bereit
Fünf eingereiste russische Arbeiterinnen grundieren
Die riesige sibirische Leinwand Ikonen-Rezepte
Die erste Fassung 1:10, so hätte der Staat
Verfahren sollen, bevor man sich ans Volk wagt
Den großen Gegenstand, den man beherrschen muß
Er bringt sich in Stimmung mit einer *Verspottung*
Des Ablaßhändlers. Russische Farben *Grüne Erde, unvergleichlich*
90 000 Tuben Fünfzehn Gehilfen Die Ewigkeit
Ein Narr im Staatsauftrag. *Ich male ins Blaue hinein*
Jedenfalls frühbürgerlich, Lanzen Spieße Sensen
Die Farbe *im Auftrag* auftragen, nein *schlagen*, wie Schneeflocken
Die Leinwand belebt sich, nicht drei nicht dreißig
Figuren, die ein Minister durchmustern könnte, dreitausend
Treten aus dem Grund, als wenn Sibirien noch einmal
Besiedelt würde und der Permafrost taut. Bauernhaufen
Fürstenheere, ein Zeitalter hingewürfelt
Szene um Szene Momente Einzelheiten Ein Traumfeld
Unter dem Regenbogen. Monster Maschinen Ein Fisch
Wie ein Raumschiff hält zwischen Abgrund und Aufstand, und er
Der durch das Bild geht (der Narr) mit weißem Gesicht
Inmitten der Aufgeregten und Aufgehängten.
Die ganze prekäre Masse, Landlose Flüchtlinge

Big Screen

Like a small untidy kingdom, this artist
In 1976, divorce moving out chaos But a prince
Can change his abode, Frankenhausen
A large commission *Early-bourgeois Revolution*, that is
Paint an epoch (that was the unit of measure)
So that the population will fit into the picture.
The rotunda stands ready like a trap
Five female workers, travelled in from Russia, settle
The proportions for the images on the vast Siberian screen
In the first version 1:10, so the state
Should have proceeded, before daring to approach the people
The large subject which they must get on top of
He warms up with a *mockery of the Seller
Of Indulgences*. Russian colours *Green earth, incomparable*
90,000 tubes Fifteen assistants Eternity
A fool with a state commission. *I paint into the blue*
Or at least early-bourgeois, lances spears scythes
Apply the colour *as per the commission*, no *beat* it, like snowflakes
The screen comes to life, not three not thirty
Figures which a minister could assess, three thousand
Step out of the background as though Siberia
Were being settled again and the permafrost is melting. Troops
Of peasants, princes' armies, an epoch cast like dice
Scene by scene Moments Details A dream field
Under the rainbow. Monster machines A fish
Like a space ship halts between the abyss and the uprising and he
(The Fool) who passes through the picture with a white face
In the midst of the agitated and the hanged.
The whole precarious mass, refugees without a land
As though squeezed out of the tube within the building

Wie aus der Tube gequetscht in dem Bau, das wäre
Der Aufenthaltsraum für die *Hellen Haufen* gewesen
Wenn sie gekämpft hätten auf dem historischen Boden
Schlachtberg *Blutrinne*, gegen die Truppen der Treuhand.
Die letzte Lücke im Bild für den *Schuh des Schmeichlers*
Den er im Nacken spürt Dann ist die Fahne
Fertig und die Staatsmacht am Ende
Der marode Maler der kaputte Staat
Steigen erschöpft von der Leiter resp. Tribüne
Macht Macht Macht Es ist lächerlich Zehn Jahre
War ich aus der Wirklichkeit ausgetreten
Wie das Volk im Jahr 89 wie um ihr
Ein Denkmal zu setzen mit dem friedlichen Aufruhr.
Mit wankenden Knien, Blutgeruch (Terpentin)
Seh ich den Maler nach der Knochenarbeit
An der Leinwand entlanggehn, die zerbrochene
Hand wischt über das Weiß einer Wange
Und er hockt sich hin und setzt sein Signum
Unter die Welt.

That would have been the green room for the *bright troops*
If they had fought on that historical ground
Battle Mountain *blood groove*, against Treuhand's troops.
The last gap in the picture for the *shoe of the flatterer*
Which he feels on his neck Then the flag
Is ready and the power of the state at an end
The marauder painter the clapped-out state
Climb exhausted down from the ladder, or rather the tribunal
Power power power It is laughable For ten years
I was absent from reality
Like the people in 1989 how to raise around it
A memorial with the peaceful insurrection.
With shaky legs, smell of blood (turpentine)
I see the painter after that hard labour
Walking along the screen, his broken hand
Wipes across the white of a cheek
And he crouches down and puts his signature
Under the world.

Geisterstunde

Als die Nacht kam, eben noch lesbar
Die Grabsteine, begannen die Toten zu reden
Mit unsern Zungen, welche ihnen fehlen
Und das Gedächtnis, bei dem Mangel an Eingeweiden
So daß wir ihnen beisprangen:
                                    darauf kam Hensel
Die die Kadaver verteilte, während wir die Zitate herauszogen –
»Man hat noch gewisse Möglichkeiten«
Schaudern! Wunder! Teschke las Arendt
Völker sprach Mann, den tot Hergebrachten
Tragelehn Brecht, den er aber kannte und darum
Nichts hermachte. Laabs gab Hilbig in verbesserter Mundart
Lammert Hermlin, den Unnachahmlichen
Gröschner: Zweig Arnold, der sich ohnehin hatte auf seinem
      Sofa vorlesen lassen.
Und mit kleinen Schritten, jedes Tier kann es
Ging Eine um, die ganz hintenhin geraten ist
Wundgelegen. Unheimlicher Ort
Wir gerade noch atmend haben sie alle zu Grabe getragen
Und erwarten ein Gleiches. Seghers mit militärischen Ehren
Abgefertigt, das Volk verbannt an die Pforte
Mir schossen die Tränen Oder Mayer der Außenseiter
Kam wieder rüber inn Osten
Weil ihm in Ewigkeit im Westen nicht wohl war.
Hacks liegt nicht hier weil Müller hier liegt
Mickel ordnete an: Nicht in die Sichtachse!
Kirsch der Kopist hat beizeiten einen Stein aufgearbeitet
Müller gab Gold für Eisen das der Rost frißt
Grashof machte einen Witz: Tabori im Abgas.
Die Chausseestraße lauschte, Hegel:

Hour of the Ghosts

When night came, the grave stones
Just about still legible, the dead began to speak
With our tongues, which they lack
And memory, for want of bowels
So that we came to their aid:
                        then Hensel arrived
And she distributed the corpses while we pulled out the quotations –
'We do still have certain possibilities'
Horrors! Miracles! Teschke read Arendt
Völker spoke Mann, brought hither dead
Tragelehn Brecht whom he knew and so
Made nothing up. Laabs gave Hilbig in an improved dialect
Lammert Hermlin, the inimitable
Gröschner: Zweig Arnold who always did have his own work
       read out to him while he lay on the sofa.
And with small steps, any animal can do it
One woman walked there who got right to the back
And was all awry and in pain. Eerie place
We still just about breathing carried them all to their graves
And expect the same. Seghers dispatched
With military honours, the people banished to the gate
Tears came to eyes Or Mayer the outsider
Came back to the East
Because in the West for eternity he was uncomfortable
Hacks isn't here because Müller is
Mickel gave the order: Not in the angle of vision!
Kirsch the copyist had in good time worked up a stone
Müller gave gold for iron that rust eats
Grashof made a joke: Tabori in the exhaust fumes.
The Chausseestrasse was listening, Hegel:

Das Wahre ist das Ganze, und hob das Wort auf
Dreck im Ohr, Dialektik Det Janze
Ist nicht det Wahre. Die Toten lebendig
Wir Gespenster, durch den Efeu schleichend
Der Kies knirschte bei Brecht & Borsig.
Schenker absent, Altmann ersetzte ihn Wenn er
Der lebend schon Ungeheure, geblasen
Hätte, Wunder! Schrecken, das hätten wir alle
Nicht überlebt und freiwillig, mit der Posaune
Ausgeatmet –

What is true is the whole, and cancelled the utterance
Dirt in his ears, dialectic What is whole
Is not the truth. The dead alive
We ghosts creeping through the ivy
The gravel grated near Brecht & Borsig.
Schenker absent, Altmann replaced him If he
Monstrous even in life, had
Blown, miracles! horrors, none of us
Would have survived it and willingly with the trumpet
Breathed out –

Notes

Some of these poems, or early versions of them, were first published in *Modern Poetry in Translation* and *Raceme*.

A Waking Dream
Schanzenviertel is a popular counter-cultural district of Hamburg. Westhofen is the fictitious concentration camp in which Anna Seghers locates her novel *The Seventh Cross*. The name alludes to the real camp, Osthofen, near Worms. Vorkuta was a Soviet Labour Camp, 1932–62. Detlev Karsten Rohwedder (1932–61) was a German politician and manager who oversaw the privatization of state-owned GDR holdings prior to reunification. He was assassinated by a sniper. The Red Army Faction claimed responsibility but the killer was never identified.

After Our Time
Two fishermen discovered the yacht in February 2016 and in the radio room, slumped over a desk, the mummified body of a German sailor by the name of Manfred Fritz Bajorat.

Catarrhsis
Leaden Union, normally Eisern Union (Iron Union), Berlin football team. 'Halt. Who's there', from *Hamlet*. The soup kitchen stands in here for 'Die Tafel' an open kitchen for the poor in Germany. 'Having none hath no care', from Pound, *Canto* CVIII. One in four is dying, allegedly, of those aged over 80 infected with the corona virus. 'The scientists are in terror', Pound, *Canto* CXV.

Wind Citizens
'Windbürgergeld' [literally wind citizen money] was a controversial bonus proposed by the SPD in Germany in 2020 to encourage citizens to allow the erection of wind turbines in their neighbourhood. The adjective 'windig' means windy but also dodgy or fly by night. 'As if on a holiday' and 'all-present, in light embrace' come from Hölderlin's unfinished Pindaric poem, 'Wie wenn am Feiertage...' [As if on Holidays] (1800). Virus is Covid-

19, the pandemic which reached Europe in March 2020. 'The green casque has outdone your elegance', Pound, *Canto LXXXI*. 'A handful of maxims' and 'a beaten path', both from Frank Raddatz's '13 Theses on the Theatre of the Anthropocene' (2020). 'How dare you', from Greta Thunberg's furious speech at the UN Climate Summit, 23 September 2019.

Gorse. Plantagenet
'Enter Rumour', *Henry IV Part II*. Donna Haraway: roughly (and blasphemously) what she said in her 'Cyborg Manifesto', in *The Socialist Review*, 1985.

Palaver in the Sand
The poem 'Material Burghammer' appeared in Braun's collection Der *Stoff zum Leben 2* [The Stuff of Life 2] originally 1982. The italicised terms are lines from this poem. *Bodenloser Satz,* literally 'groundless sentence', is the playful title of a work published by Braun in 1990 reflecting on the ecological demise of the GDR and using his characteristic archaeological process. The Book Sheikh is Dr Ali bin Tamim, Head of the Abu Dhabi Center for the Arab Language.

The Leper
Rudolf Bahro, the cultural philosopher who was imprisoned in Bautzen, a notorious prison for political prisoners in the GDR, 1978-9. *The Logic of Salvation* is Bahro's book, *Logik der Rettung,* which appeared in 1987.

Cares of the Body Politic
'More than we think, we are', from the poem 'Libation' by Karl Mickel, 1973.

Handshake
Günter Wallraff, writer and undercover journalist who reported on the working conditions of Turkish guestworkers in West Germany in the 1980s. Vaucluse. Petrarch famously loved his Laura in the Vaucluse valley; and in 'a green inwardly wood' we see one of many of Braun's own self-citations from his published *Work Journal*.

Aggregate K
AGGREGAT K is a group of graphic script-works by Carlfriedrich Claus from Annaberg in the Harz Mountains, 1986-88. The poem enters into the concepts of his thought-landscapes. 'Around which all revolves as around the sun': cf. 'Society simply will not find its equilibrium until it revolves around the sun of labour' – Karl Marx, 'Epilogue to Revelations Concerning the Communist Trial in Cologne' (anon, 1853). '[N]o qiángjiān, no shǒuyín': no raping, no wanking. 'Djin': compare Braun's poem 'Überleb los' [Survive go /Surlife less], written 1988 in connection with his collection *Die Zickzackbrücke* [The Zigzag Bridge], 1992 and published in his *Texte in zeitlicher Folge*, 9, 1992. 'Brothers, to the sun, to freedom' is the title of the German re-writing of the Russian work song 'Brave, comrades, in step!', and one of the most famous workers' songs in East Germany.

Sixth Circle
Jens Braun, born 1962, read Economics at the University of Leipzig. In 1990, without a job, he refused state benefits and went for a while 'into an affordable exile'. He died in 2015. The Granua is a tributary of the Danube. Marcus Aurelius was there campaigning against the German tribes (and writing his *Meditations*).

Bodily Proof
Bornholmer was a border-crossing between East and West Berlin, the first to be opened on 9 November 1989. 'Was it by destiny or chance', *Inferno* XXXII, 76. 'Which had clouded ... in the morning light', *Purgatory* I, 18, 20. 'We know full well that faith was a stranger to you'. This alludes to Braun's own poem 'Inferno IV. Limbus' and to *Purgatory* XX, 59, in his *Handbibliothek der Unbehausten* [Travelling Library of the Dispossessed] (2016). Commandante, alludes both to Dante and to Hugo Chávez who assumed that title. '[T]he pole/ Leafing green', Braun saw this surviving tree in Hiroshima in 2002. Ann, the poet Ann Cotton. 'Not the sweet/ and bitter, but steadfast language' – Braun ascribes these lines to her.

K Like Kertész
12 October. Braun's note: 2001. The quotations – italicized – are from *Letzte Einkehr* [Final taking stock], the diary of the Hungarian author Imre Kertész (1929-2016). He won the Nobel Prize in 2002.

Anatomy. Kleist, Meinhof
Braun brings Heinrich von Kleist (1777–1811), the writer, and Ulrike Meinhof (1934–76), radical political activist, into a glancing sort of connection. He shot himself on the Wannsee, she committed suicide (or was murdered, some say) in her cell in Stammheim Prison. Both were, differently, extremists. Kleist's essay 'On the gradual production of thoughts whilst speaking' is applied to Meinhof's beginning to understand what 'needs doing' in the very process of unclearly taking action. *konkret* was a radically left-wing magazine begun by Meinhof's husband Klaus Rainer Röhl in 1957. She wrote regularly for it. Andreas Baader (1943-77) was co-founder with Meinhof of the Red Army Faction. Like her, he died in Stammheim, in a suicide pact or, some say, was murdered. Leyden jar: also called the Kleist jar (Braun calls it that), after Ewald Georg von Kleist, who invented it, in 1745, as a means storing electricity. His invention was taken up and developed in Leyden, hence its more usual name. Prrinzzing: Theodor Prinzing, controversial prosecutor of the RAF in the Stammheim trial 1974–77.

Cyborg
Donna Haraway is the author of 'A Cyborg Manifesto', published 1985 in *Socialist Review*. Victory over the flesh: Braun notes, 'A whole industry is dreaming of victory over the flesh'. He has in mind Martine Rothblatt, Founder and CEO of United Therapeutics. She is the author of *From Transgender to Transhuman*.

Stone Rubbing
Zhao Tingyang, Braun calls him the most influential of China's new philosophers. Hubert Robert (1733-1808) a French Romantic painter known especially for semi-fictitious depictions of ruins in Italy and France. Carl Schmitt (1888-1985), jurist, political theorist,

prominent Nazi. For Schmitt, the political was reducible to the existential distinction between friend and enemy. Tianxia, literally 'all under one heaven', is the idea of an inclusive and harmonious world for all. Age of Zhou: Zhou Enlai, first President of the People's Republic of China (1949–76). Age of Xi: Xi Yinping, the current President (since 2013). 'The Doubter', a poem by Brecht in praise of productive doubt. Demolished/ demolition men, alludes to Brecht's poem 'Questions of a worker who reads'.

Big Screen

The poem celebrates the opening, in 1989, of Werner Tübke's monumental work *Frühbürgerliche Revolution in Deutschland* [Early-bourgeois revolution in Germany]. 1989 was the 500th anniversary of the birth of Thomas Müntzer, a radical theologian and the leader in the Peasants' War. He was executed in 1525. The 'bright troops' alludes to Braun's own story, *Die Hellen Haufen* (2011) in which a mass revolt of the dispossessed is imagined. Treuhand was an agency set up in June 1990 to privatize previously state-owned companies prior to the re-unification of East and West Germany in October.

Hour of the Ghosts

When night came: The location of this wake is the Dorotheenfriedhof in Berlin during the night of 9–10 June 2017. Living writers come together and by naming and reading the dead and buried there, keep them alive. Braun's friend and fellow-poet Karl Mickel had himself published a volume called *Geisterstunde* [Hour of the Ghosts] in 1999, the year before he died. 'One woman walked there ...': Ruth Berlau, Brecht's unhappy lover. Braun's contemporary, Heiner Müller (1929–1995) chose a grave marker made of iron, designed eventually to disappear, eaten by rust.